AF582690

The Story of
My Encounter
With High
Witchcraft Powers
A True Story of an African
Experience in the Mangrove
Rain Forest
W.I. Joseph
Revised Edition

The Story of My Encounter with High Witchcraft Powers

A True Story of an African Experience in the Mangrove Rain Forest

BY

W.I. JOSEPH

A Must Read Story

For Believers and Non Believers

On High Witchcraft Operations

The Story of My Encounter with High Witchcraft Powers

Revised Edition

ISBN: 979-884-750-0821

All scripture quotations are taken from King James Version of the Holy Bible except otherwise stated.

DEDICATION

I dedicate this book to God Almighty and my entire reading audience.

Thank You Holy Spirit for preserving my life through this valley of death experience. I am forever grateful and indebted to You.

TABLE OF CONTENTS

ABOUT THE BOOK

The book is about a true life story of the beginning of my ministerial calling, ministry and later encounters with high Witchcraft Powers as I stepped into the office of my calling and operations.

Here, the story portrayed my ministry in it's formative stage, processes, encounters and transitions into hierarchy of spiritual power and authority. At each transition, it brought about an incredibly increased power and authority to deal with powers from the dark world - Satan.

The story conveyed truth about the existence of witchcraft, occult and wicked powers in this world. Their presence is real and everywhere imagined and unimagined.

But much more real is the presence and power of God, shielding his children in all circumstances they may find themselves.

Also, some godly counsels at the end of the book for everyone to adhere to and stay safe.

Go ahead and get inside the book to find out more; don't be told!

ABOUT THE AUTHOR

Apostle W.I. Joseph is an anointed man of God. He's gifted with revelation and wisdom of God's truth, called by God and given the mandate of liberating people by the preaching of the gospel.

He's anointed to reveal God's truth and power through his teachings, writings, healing and deliverance services and crusades.

His ministry is characterize with signs and wonders and has brought great healings and deliverances with prophetic words and direction to many across the globe and still counting.

W.I Joseph is married to Pastor (Mrs.) Gloria Joseph, and the union is blessed with two beautiful anointed kids: Shepherd and Emmanuelle as at the time of writing this book.

BIOGRAPHY OF MY CALL

It was on a cool morning, I woke up not feeling to go to work but to work from home since I only had few business proposals to put up; and also work on one or two financial tenders for submission the next working day. My wife got set for work and I bid her farewell. I quickly fixed some pressing chores then came back to settle on my computer to begin my work for the day. But I felt this burden to pray on certain issues and intercede for some set of people. So, I left the computer system and went and lied on the tiled floor in the sitting room and began to pray; asking the Lord to move on behalf of these ones. All of a sudden, I went into a trance. I saw myself moving on what looked like road towards a hilltop or better still mountain. Ahead was a single giant tree that looks evergreen, no any other tree or shrub near to it. While I was still moving, then a lady walk passed me; I quickly noticed she wasn't alright. But she kept pacing ahead of me; then I heard a mighty voice from above telling me to deliver her. As I moved towards carrying out the instruction, she took off and ran of my sight into one meandering gully erosion gulf. I started off to run after her to bring her back; but I heard the same voice asking me to stop and command her to come back to where I was instead. Quickly, I stopped and commanded her as I was instructed; then reluctantly here comes she. I stretched forth my right hand towards her and commanded those demons to leave her! Instantly, she collapsed to the ground. I went close to her and touched her by the head and declared her free in Jesus name. She immediately stood up and began to shout and confirm her healing and deliverance. She was deaf and dump, had cancer, and many other infirmities I couldn't remember now; all gone and perfectly healed.

After this happened, I heard a majestic thunderous voice quaking in the heavenly, this time I looked up and saw with my eyes the voice of God moving in the air as a mighty wave of the sea; just as it is written in **Psalms 29:3-4 (KJV)**

3 The voice of the Lord is upon the waters: the God of glory thundereth: the Lord is upon many waters.

4 The voice of the Lord is powerful; the voice of the Lord is full of majesty.

He called out my name – Wilfred… today I have called you and ordained you as one of my prophets and enlists you among my ministers. And other things He said which I may not say, then I responded with a loud AAAAAAAMEN! And came out of the trance.

This happened in late 2017.

Beloved, it was more than real.

Shortly after this encounter, I went on my normal evangelism routines to a neighborhood hospital. There I saw the raw miracle power of God performed through my very hands. A lady that was brought to the hospital for whatever illness I cannot tell, was dripped with water and other treatments administered on her: she could not sit left alone walking at the moment. She looks pale and flaccid. I took one of her hands and prayed for her and thereafter, I asked her to stand; the parents were skeptical at initial but she immediately sat up and also began walking. Hallelujah! It was marvelous in our sight.

This marks the beginning of miracles, signs and wonders ministry for me shortly after.

To God be the glory!

by donating any amount to support my free books publishing project.

Thank you!

WILFRED IORHEMBA JOSEPH

This is part of my evangelism and capacity building project for the body of Christ Jesus world wide. My books are made completely FREE.

Together, let's do this for Christ.

PLEASE CHECK THE DONATION PAGE

Passionate Appeal!

Please I humbly and passionately invite your gracious support and donation to help my free books publishing. I have a passion to build a free online books for global consumption.

Please support this noble course to help pay for quality proof reading and editing before publishing.

As you do so, may you be richly blessed.

W.I Joseph

Please for more info contact

 fredwil07@yahoo.com

 +2348151887054

 Agwan Gede Kwotto Nasarawa State - Nigeria

 www.sfe.org.ng

For Support/ Donation

Use any of the below mediums convenient for you.

Perfect Money® Just perfect

U38877935
E39282756
G38563264

PAYEER®
P1076792383

WebMoney Sapienti sat

WMID: 285662555478
USERNAME: +2348029192303

Payoneer
fredwil2013@gmail.com

NETELLER

fredwil2013@gmail.com

WESTERN UNION WU

Wilfred Iorhemba Joseph
fredwil2013@gmail.com

Acct Name: Wilfred Joseph Iorhemba
Acct Number: 2237953216
Bank Name: United Bank for Africa -UBA
Location: Nasarawa - Nigeria

MoneyGram. money transfer

Wilfred Iorhemba Joseph
08029192303
Or
United Bank for Africa -UBA
Bank code: 033362087
Nasarawa - Nigeria

Please if you use Western Union, MoneyGram or Ria, endeavor to send me your donation details through this email fredwil2013@gmail.com

INTRODUCTION

The Story of My Encounter with High Witchcraft Powers is a true and real life event that took place in my early years of ministry, in a village called **Uyenu** in Nasarawa Local Government Area, Nasarawa State - Nigeria.

This story is a reaffirmation and attestation to the fact that, witchcraft is real; and the presence of witches and wizards and spiritual wicked powers is certain, especially to those who seems to differ or take a neutral ground on the existence of Witchcraft.

The story you are about to hear will shock you; add to your knowledge, and at the same time, open you up to the reality of Witchcraft world; and also increase your understanding of the operations of these powers and their kingdom activities. (Only if you're new or unfamiliar with this knowledge and experiences).

The world we are living in is so spiritual; and largely governed by high spiritual authorities: be it from God or Satan.

The earth is like a showroom where activities of the spirit realms are being showcased daily. And the spirit realm is the workshop where the main activities are being initiated, fashioned and fabricated. But have no showroom, hence the earth becomes the choice place. If you're thinking that things happening here on earth starts from the earth, you're mistaken the whole setup. You've got to understand that, whatever that will exist here on earth must first subsist in the realms of the spirit or spiritual world.

Therefore, take back your sit and enjoy your read.

Chapter One

THE MAN BEHIND THE ENCOUNTER

Wilfred Iorhemba Joseph is a man helped by God.

He's an anointed preacher of the gospel of Christ Jesus. Called by God and given the mandate of healing the sick, and setting the captives free from the cruel shackles of Satan.

Upon his being called by God into ministry; he started out on mission work in one local interior village where there was scarcely social amenities, having left township where he enjoyed good amenities and standard of living.

All these happened to prove his genuine calling by God that he must be humbled and experience hardships to become more mature for the task ahead.

Prior to his calling as an apostle of Christ Jesus, he was into Business Management Consultancy and also, contracts. But his calling stripped him off this lucrative venture into harsher lonely prayerful lifestyle that is geared towards building and enhancing his spiritual authority and capability for the job.

Sooner, his encounters with the spirit world begin to prove the essence and benefits of his harsh training from God. The story under view is one of the evidences of this harsh trainings. And it's yielding positive results.

W. I. Joseph is happily married to pastor Gloria and the union is blessed with two kids at the time of writing this book.

Chapter Two

HOW IT ALL STARTED

The work of the ministry is a dangerous one especially one that is based in creative miracles and wonders. I heard some theological exegeses well meaning, but on the contrary, tactically misleading on the topic of deliverance in ministry. Watch this, the concept of deliverance i.c exorcism shouldn't be subjected to theological debate as that can substantially creates potent gateway for Satan to thrive in people's lives. I mean, some people find solace in criticizing power ministry. This shouldn't be so.

Deliverance in ministry is more of healing ministry and prophetic, miracles, signs and wonders. How come someone somewhere because of his theological prowess will now begin to confuse others about the existence of deliverance in ministry?

Beloved, please don't be confused!

This encounter is a product of deliverance in ministry that God entrust in my hands; I cherished and appreciate Him for it daily. I can't questioned God just the way Job did not questioned Him having received the multiple evil reports that befell him in a day.

Please pardon my emotions if I sounded unethical and rude. It's the holy anger just welling up from within when people are not careful in marking their limit as men but hastily run to conclude what God has not told them neither instructed. Zeal without knowledge is vain, and effort in futility. So be warn!

Now back to the story.

In the year 2018 precisely on April 28th, having received my call from God in 2017; I packed my bags and luggage to a place where I knew nothing about. And a tribe that is strange to me, except that I was being led by the Spirit of God. As at the time of leaving for the mission field, I had ran out of cash and my account was in red. I have to sell some of my electronics and home appliances like laptops, fridge, blender to mention a few; just to raise the money I needed for the relocation. At this point, Satan was preaching many wonderful sermons which seems true to me. But God constrained me and was with me otherwise I would have considered the satanic sermons.

These were his deceptive sermons: if God called you, He would have provided the money for your relocation don't you think so? Because Satan don't always run at conclusion like humans do. He will always seek your opinion for you to run the conclusion so you will think it's your decision. At other time, he will ask, are you sure God called you to do what you are about to do? Leaving room yet for me to run the conclusion. At another time, he used my business associate and a bosom friend of mine to harassed the day light out of me. And very many tempting sermons just for me to stay back and disobey

God. But glory to God in the highest, I didn't to the detriment of Satan and to my security and blessings.

Having said that, my family and I landed at our new place of assignment. We packed into one rented apartment that was haphazardly built without completion. I pleaded with my wife to accept this new challenge as a fate of love. At beginning, it was not easy, a daunting task indeed, but God intervened and helped us in familiarizing and acclimatizing through Holy Ghost adaptation mechanism.

The first sign we saw while there was warm acceptance by the people. The people of the place gave us a right hand of fellowship. They accepted the gospel of Christ we brought but not without challenges.

Another sign was God miraculously gave my wife a teaching job in a private nursery and primary school there. While we were yet rejoicing over that, another job landed on me at one private secondary school as a subject teacher on contract basis. The interesting side of these jobs was, we did not apply for either of it but God supernaturally provided and used it to sustain us while working for Him. Hence, we were not begging or depending on the people. And this gave us great relief as our basic financial needs were met without owing or borrowing.

This miracle alone reassured me of God's guidance and leadership in my ministry. And it was a major motivation and encouragement. Because I pleaded with Him not to allow me to become a burden to my converts. But instead, let me have to support when the need arises. And He answered me so quickly beyond my expectations. Just as stated in the below scriptures:

Isaiah 65:24 And it shall come to pass, that before they call, I will answer; and while they are yet speaking, I will hear.

Ephesians 3:20 Now unto him that is able to do exceeding abundantly above all that we

ask or think, according to the power that worketh in us.

So, the training began. I started evangelism and prayer outreaches and began to get converts on daily and weekly basis. Soon, we got a little hall in a government secondary school - their Fellowship of Christian Students (FCS) building. We started our weekly activities there. As time progressed, the Holy Spirit led in my heart to start praying in tongues, that is, in the spirit for hours daily. It was a good challenge for me. So, without hesitation, I stepped out in faith and began to pray for hours in tongues. I started by praying for one hour daily. Then it increased to two, three, four, five, six and seven hours progressively, a day for weeks and months. Then another challenge came for me to move to 24 hours a day praying in tongues. I must say that, these transitional trainings were not easy and left little to be desired of but God was fully behind me.

Before this training exercises, I had no courage to pray for anyone and lay hands where necessary. I could only do a general prayer. And I had not started deliverance prayers for people because one, I have not yet received the enabling of the Spirit. And secondly, I do not possessed the boldness to pray demons and situations out of people's lives.

But while the training got to its peak, God supernaturally arranged a prayer meeting organized by one apostle; where I was invited as a guest minister. Some traveling guest preachers were also invited to the prayer program. I had never laid my hands on anyone while praying for them in public. And I had never prophesy before in public.

But during this prayer meeting, the gift and power of God begin to manifest in me. I prophesied and also laid hands on people while praying for them. Each one I laid hands on; falls out under God's power, and miracles were taking place. Before long, people noticed the power of God on me, they started deserting other ministers and insisted that I pray for them. Glory to God who made it possible.

This meeting opened me up to the supernatural; and the spiritual investment of God in me at this point was revealed. That means, I can begin to pray for people as He demonstrated through me this day. And so I continued.

From that day forward, my ministry stepped into a new dimension of operating in the spirit.

I must say that, I was not a pastor before, never pastored any church either. And none of my family members was a minister of the gospel neither is. So, God just called me as a fresher and started off with me as a beginner; and He's giving me the requisite trainings that will help my ministry to succeed.

Having said that, I began to experience a new challenge as I stepped into my office of calling. Many attacks from the kingdom of darkness begin to come in against me. At first, I was totally confused and don't know what to do next. But while I turned to my sufficient and timely helper - the Holy Spirit, He encouraged me to double up my prayer life and devotion to God.

One of the very first attacks I experienced was, when I conducted deliverance on a particular family, the family ancestral alter demons came after me. This was how it happened. When I came in contact with these demons, I saw the chiefest sat down at a milling machine, while the remaining three were working on the mill. Guess what they were working on? Substance that looks like rice. This family was labouring to get the rice-like substance, and whatever they got, they will bring it to the milling machine only for those demons to mill everything and at the end of refinement, for them to take back; the chiefest demon will instruct the other demons to scatter everything and that's exactly what they will do. Then this family will have to go back empty. I stood and watched this circle of action by the demons repeated itself on two occasions. When the third was about to take place, I interjected and asked the demons to stop! The chiefest demon asked me, who sent you and what concern you with whatever we're doing? I responded, yes it concerns me because this family are now for Christ and they must be delivered. The demons replied me, no way! I also responded, then stop right now! Before long, we engaged in a combat and one of the demons threw what looks like a stone at me, and it landed on my mouth top lips. I also got back at them in a very hurtful way.

Now let me explain the implication here for better understanding. What I saw and my encounter with this ancestral family demons is a replica of what was happening to this family physically. They will work very hard but get little in return or sometime next to nothing. They're farmers by occupation. In the village, people knew them as suffer-heads: that's family that work without results or benefits. Even they themselves got use to it.

The Holy Spirit later revealed to me that it was the family ancestral demons that were responsible for destroying their efforts, just as I was opportune to see in the spirit as narrated above. These demons wouldn't let them achieve anything reasonable enough to help themselves.

Again, the stone like object the demons threw at me that got me on my mouth; two days later turned to a serious injury on my mouth. I suffered with the pains for some weeks before it finally got healed but left a scar on my mouth till date. This is one of the hazards of deliverance because at times, there are come back attacks to hurt you.

The good thing about this first experience was, I quickly learnt my lesson and outgrew such further attacks. How? By knowing what to do in such situations and not acting ignorantly. The reason the demons got me was, first, I was immature and inexperienced in the act of deliverance or exorcism especially family deliverance. It was much later that I discovered; actually this family had the ancestral demonic alter in their late father's house. So, the first step was to lead the family to renounce or repudiate their allegiance to this alter and demons. Then next step would have being to destroy the family ancestral demonic alter before lastly conducting a family deliverance on them.

But I rather moved with passion and zeal to conduct deliverance while family ancestral demonic alter was still standing. This was why I got hurt.

But I am grateful to Jesus for not allowing me to be consumed in the process because, many lost their lives in the same process. Remember, Satan always capitalized on our ignorance to hurt us.

Hosea 4:6 My people are destroyed for lack of knowledge: because thou hast rejected knowledge, I will also reject thee, that thou shalt be no priest to me: seeing thou hast forgotten the law of thy God, I will also forget thy children.

Chapter Three

THE ENCOUNTER WITH THE HIGH WITCHCRAFT POWERS

In the winter of year 2020, another family met me over an issue of incessant and frequent death occurence in their family. Through the prophetic gifting and grace upon me, I told them, they need a serious family deliverance. Because what was responsible for the death in their family was a strong evil alter. And they confirmed it to be true. One of the victim family members said, there is an occult and witchcraft alter belonging to their late father. And now the mother has inherited it taken over. I sent for the mother and preached Christ to her. She accepted and received Him as her Lord and savior. I proceeded further to advise her against destroying that alter. She told me the witchcraft alter was a large family thing, so let her consult with all the concerned elders and authorities to seek their consent. I obliged her request.

She left, and did all her consultations and got back to me after a few weeks time with the news that, the authorities have her permission to go ahead and destroy the alters. Because it was in three places: one in the house, second in the forest, and the last in the river.

Look at the strategic locations of these alters. One was located in the forest, east region; the second which was the main shrine at home; and the last one in the river, located in the west region. My God, can you imagine it. Alright! Behind their permission was a set up to take my life in exchange for their witchcraft practices. Because, this witchcraft was in the highest ranking in their entire clan and ethnicity.

I prayed and prepared myself. We fixed the date of destroying the alters. Graciously, the day came and we set out, went and destroyed successful the three shrines. Thereafter, I conducted deliverance upon all the family members.

But because of the severity of the witchcraft network, I have to reschedule a date for the final prayer of consecration and victory over the witchcraft kingdom.

To my surprise, when the day came for their final prayers, only some family members showed up leaving behind the main person concerned - the woman who was handling the shrines after the demise of her husband.

I told the family members present the implication of leaving the woman out of this final prayers and they concord that I should go ahead and complete the prayers. So, we did the prayers and they all left rejoicing.

Something happened remarkably, the people that were scheduled to die automatically escape death arrows that were shot at them in the realms of the spirit.

One pregnant woman amongst them was given different prophecies that she must die with the pregnancy during childbirth or labor. Fear was all over her because she knew what was happening in their family.

But glory to God in the highest; God came through for her and saved her life and that of her unborn child. When her delivery time came, she delivered successfully a healthy bouncing baby girl at home. Glory!

This is the God we serve. A merciful loving father that cares for his suffering children.

Chapter Four

THE DAY OF VISITATION

It was exactly around 12:00am I was in my prayer room on my knees praying to my Father in heaven, thanking Him and also reminding Him of His promises over my life.

I was desiring more of Him because that's all that matters to me anytime any moment. I don't wish to live a minute without Him and his consciousness. As my conversations continue with God, at about 1:00am on the dot I felt a divine torch and not too long, power flow all over me. I began to marinate in His presence and glory. The hand of the Lord became so strong on me, I could only pray less at this point but rejoice more. I began to tell the Lord not to stop, neither should He go! Let's continue because I was really enjoying the ecstasy of His glory. Dear friend, when you experience the glory of God, you will never wish it ends. You won't desire anything more than Him. His glory will strip you off yourself and bring you to a place of real intimacy, fellowship and worship.

I then turned around and found His angel standing by me that very moment, empowering my body, soul and spirit ahead of what was to come shortly. And when I saw him, we both smile and he disappeared leaving me alone. This happened just to strengthen me the way the angel of God came and strengthened Jesus Christ before his crucifixion.

Luke 22:43 And there appeared an angel unto him from heaven, strengthening him.

Immediately the angel of God was gone, here come two men. I asked them who are you; and what do you want? They replied, we have come to bring you along with us to our master, he sents us. As they began to speak, I noticed, power exhuming out of them, trying to hypnotize me. Hence, I obliged their demand. We set out and began to fly in the air. This happened physically, I wasn't sleeping, neither will I tag it: out of body experience. No! I was fully aware of everything that was happening around and within me.

So we flew thousands of kilometers away from the village into some thick mangrove rain forests. I kept wondering, what the hell in the world is happening; where are we going? But I just kept following because I was under instruction to come. While we were going, there was only one thought that kept resonating in my spirit which is: to destroy their temple and all that there's to them.

After flying for like half an hour, we finally arrived at a gate. When I looked around, everywhere was bushes, but here stood this tall watchtower with watchmen on it. And inside the gate was an estate with state of the art facilities such that there was none in that village. There were magnificent edifices erected there. I began to marvel at the wonders of this world. My thoughts continue to flow endlessly. So, on this earth there are other worlds only known and seeing by the highly spiritual people. God is indeed great was my conclusion.

We went through seven gigantic gates to arrived at the main shrine. At each gate, there was a tower and watch men on it, and we will be checked before granting access to pass. Even in the kingdom of darkness, there are networks of protocol.

Chapter Five

THE WITCHCRAFT KINGDOM

I got to the place and it quickly reminded me of township because, there was an estate with modern buildings such as fancy bungalows and duplexes scattered around with modern interlocking; covering the compound of each house with beautiful landscaping. It baffled me alot, bccause contrary to my opinion of what a typical witchcraft kingdom should look like, this one is unlike it. I was expecting to see thatch houses only in mud and the likes but here stood one of the very best estates even in the entire state. Anyway, travel they say, is the door to experiencing culture shock.

After taking a view of the place, I instantly knew within my spirit that, this was the headquarters of witches and wizards and occult groups in the land. For different witches and wizards and occultists travel from far and near to attend their meeting whenever they have an occasion there. I also got intelligence in the spirit that, this is where matters of destiny of the land and the people are decided, including governance.

And this time was one of such. They were preparing for a great gathering, as a result, they needed a special sacrifice to honor their invitees. Some foreign witches and wizards and occultists some time also visit the place for their international meetings.

Ahead of the estate, that is, after the seventh gate; lies their shrine. This shrine was built with red ant hill. It was in the shape of a cone-like dome. The walls were not plastered, leaving it to bear the rough surface and texture the way it was built. The structure can accommodate approximately over a thousand people.

Inside the shrine lied all kinds of charms, skulls both humans and animals, reptiles, assorted figurines and witchcraft and occult arts. The grandmaster is always there because that's his place of authority and rulership. He has messengers attending to him at all times. They're ever willing to take instructions any moment. That's their duty.

If the kingdom of darkness can be so organized; then the Kingdom of God here on earth through the church should be much more organized than they're.

Praise God!

Chapter Six

THE CONQUEST

Immediately we arrived at the shrine door, one of the emissaries asked me to wait at the door while they go in and inform their master.

They both went in. One stood by the door post inside, and the other went straight to the master and bowed his head in reverence and told the master in a cracky voice, 'we have brought the man you asked us to bring'. In response, I heard an angry deep voice that mutter words like, 'why did you bring that man here? Do you both want him to destroy this place, can't you see the fire on his head? He continued, that man carry fire. Send him back now!

At this point, I couldn't wait any longer, so I hopped into the shrine to begin my mission. I had only one wish and it was my mission: just to destroy the shrine and their master. But the two emissaries blocked me and hauled me out. I wanted to resist their attempt to avert the battle, but I heard a voice within that said, since they couldn't do anything to you, just leave them and go. And I obeyed.

They had planned to use me for their sacrifice because I destroyed one of their strong shrines in a strategic location. So they planned to use my blood for sacrifice to rebuild the shrine. But glory to God for He knows exactly what was about to come, so He sent His angel to fortify me against such attack. And indeed, they lost the battle. Glory!

This is why the scripture says, 'by strength shall no man prevail'. Please read again for yourself.

1 Samuel 2:9 He will keep the feet of his saints, and the wicked shall be silent in

darkness; for by strength shall no man prevail.

You hear that. Just imagine what would've happened to me if God had not fortified me. No one is a super human as regards to the battles between us and Satan. We all live and prevail by His grace. If Jesus Christ himself at the point of crucifixion needed divine strengthening being God in human. Then, who am I not to need one and more to stay ahead of my enemies. Wisdom is profitable to direct.

Chapter Seven

THE BATTLE DEFLATED AND AVERTED

Child of God, there is a great difference between the power of God and the power of Satan. It is good to be empowered by God. I said this with all humility and sincerity. I have nothing to boast about except God. For I am what I am by His grace.

Upon receiving the news of my presence in the witchcraft kingdom, the occult grandmaster, gave an immediate matching order that, I should be quickly evacuated, and returned back to my place. That my presence there could cause a catastrophic destruction upon their shrine and kingdom.

So, I was pushed back. I wanted to fight but I was constrained, so I refrained from exerting my wish. You must understand that, if you're genuinely called by God, and you're working with Him, you will not lack His backing and support. He will be with you always; especially in hard times.

Isaiah 43:2 When thou passest through the waters, I will be with thee; and through the rivers, they shall not overflow thee: when thou walkest through the fire, thou shalt not be burned; neither shall the flame kindle upon thee.

And so it is with everyone who is genuinely born again and walking with God.

Whenever the kingdom of darkness want to attack you, there is always a shield around you; and a mark of the blood of Jesus on your forehead, telling the enemy: torch not my anointed, and do my prophet no harm.

Except if you're living in falsehood, the kingdom of darkness can not drink your blood. Because, your blood have been mixed with that of Jesus Christ; therefore it's corrosive and bitter for the enemy to torch, let alone to drink it. To drink the blood of a believer in Christ Jesus by Satan and his demons, is synonymous to drink corrosive acid by humans. No sane person takes such substance and pleasurably drinks; expecting to have some fun or best of time. It will rather turn into a worst time instead.

You should know that the hedge of God's fire of protection is not only around you but also on you!

Finally, they succeeded in parrying away the battle they started, but it was to the glory of God.

I prophesy over your life, your enemies shall not succeed over you in Jesus Christ name.

Please permit me, for the greater is blessed by the lesser as Melchizedek blessed Abraham. That's why I prayed for you as the lesser. Not that I am more anointed than you're. Thanks for your understanding.

Chapter Eight

THE BATTLE AVERTED BUT NOT WITHOUT A SCAR

After rejecting my presence at the shrine by the occult grandmaster, I was asked to go back. I argued with them; you brought me here, how could you just say go back without leading me out? They declined and insist that I should go on my own. Alright! I replied them. If you want me out of here, then bring me out otherwise, I will remain. So it became another commotion between us.

At last, they took me out through all the gates and left me in the forest to go back. But before then, they provoked my anger, so I injured one of them with what looks like a stone. One of them first threw it at me. I in turn used it to inflict injury on him, but I was unhurt.

After they left me outside their estate, I found myself flying back home. All this happened with my consciousness intact. I wish I could explain further but words failed me for exact expression.

Dear friend, the kingdom of darkness is real; but much more real, is the Kingdom of our God.

Three days later, I received a visitation from them again, vowing to frustrate my ministry. I asked them how they were going to achieve that. Their response shocked me.

They replied, 'we will stop people from coming to your ministry'. I asked again, how? They responded, we will discourage them and they will not come to your ministry again.

Well, they did not do otherwise but exactly as they have promised. Not too long, people started leaving my ministry. They will go and join other ministries. But when they have a problem, they will run to me. And God usually intervenes when I pray for them. This circle continues for a protracted period of time.

But I did not worry, because I knew God is with me and it's just a matter of time, it shall come to pass if their strategies are exhausted.

Child of God, when you engage Satan in a battle, expect a scar. The scar will serve as a sign and reminder that God is more than Satan. Although he may have tried, but with God, you're more than a conqueror. You're not just trying to conquer but you're more than the one who conquers. Glory!

Chapter Nine

RE-RELOCATION

On December 28th 2021, my family and I re-relocated the ministry to another sub-urban city in the state. This relocation was confirmed by God because I didn't want to go without His approval.

I had fasted and prayed for this time so when it came, I was over excited to move out of that village to a new location. Not just for the sake of changing environment, but moving to a new location also means, a new higher level for our ministry.

This was a transitional transformation that can only be fathom in the spirit realm. The spiritually inclined will understand the implication of this process or action better.

Before our final moving out, I remembered when God gave me the dates for our relocation; I gladly informed our few congregants and also well wishers, that by this period, we shall be relocating the ministry. But quite unfortunate or fortunately, when the date came, we were still there. I was confused and went back to God to know why, and what's next. Only to hear a sweet comforting voice of the Father assuring me not to worry about the time and date but should just hope in him. That the time is near. But my concern was about the date I already told my members and friends, now they may doubt or question my credibility in terms of my relationship with God to access accurate information from Him.

God on the other hand, was not moved by such. You know, God is the Almighty; nothing and no one can contend with Him. What He wills, He does. And with Him, nothing is impossible. Remember the story of Jonah. Prophet Jonah didn't want to deliver God's message to the people of Nineveh because he knew; the way God gave the message; He will do directly the opposite thereby making him a false prophet. And so it happened.

Notwithstanding, I kept faith and enquired again: Lord, when will our relocation take place? This was some time in October of 2021 when I did the asking again. And He graciously reaffirmed, not far. That I should keep trusting. The question now is, what was stopping or impeding our moving? Simple, finance!

Exactly, on December 15th, 2021 God spoke to two different individuals: a man and a woman not even in my country - Nigeria where I reside. The woman from the United States of America; and the man from Canada. Both gave me an offering of **Fifteen Thousand Naira (₦15,000)** each making the sum of **₦30,000** within the same period without I requesting. And this was the exact amount I needed to relocate.

At this time, my joy knew no bound. Because God did not only raised the finance but also assured me that, He's indeed the God of all flesh, and a promise keeper. He's too faithful to fail anybody. Just keep your firm trust in Him. That's all you need. Have faith in God - Jesus admonished us in Mark 11:22.

I gladly went and arranged the new place and we relocated.

Another interesting thing that happened during our relocation was this, the vehicle that conveyed our luggage did it for free! Amazing God! He's indeed the God of miracles. If we were to pay, the money wouldn't have been enough. But God supernaturally handled it. Glory!

Child of God, let me comfort you with these words. You may be passing through a difficult situation that seems as if you aren't going to come out, but that's not true! It's just for a moment. Hold onto God, let not your faith fail at this crucial time. You'll come out soon in a big way and become better off!

Chapter Ten

THE BATTLE INTENSIFIED

Having moved to our new place, I was instructed by God to pray and fast and wait upon the Lord for the period of thirty days i.e one month. I did so. I knew no one in the new location and was wondering how to start off the ministry there. But amazingly, upon finishing my indoor prayer program, God instructed me to organize a prayer in the house where we rented. I did exactly as I was told. During the prayer meeting, God's Word came forth with power, healing and deliverance and miracles took place. Before long, news of the event went round the city that, there was a new servant of God in town. And that God is using him mightily.

This was how my ministry exploded within a short period of time. People began to come from far and near. Miracles upon miracles were taking place as God was working with us and confirming His word with signs following. Every day I and my team will pray for the people from morning till night.

Souls were been added to the kingdom daily as the Lord gave the increase. It was a good experience for me and very much wonderful.

The press for word of God and miracles were becoming increasingly exponential.

We were busy with the Lord work daily.

The witchcraft kingdom of the land was irateness and in total confusion because confessions by those possessed keep flowing as we pray for the people. Once the witchcraft and occult spirits come under God's power, when asked, they will confessed all the atrocities they have committed and still committing. To add salt to injury, they will also reveal their identity by calling out names and locations. This created more upheaval. The whole city was turned upside down as news began flying around about the identity of witches and wizards in the land. Soon, people became very much aware of those who were involved in witchcraft and occultic practices.

A case of a particular sister was terrible. This sister was under the spell of her uncle. The uncle wanted her death but was afraid of killing her at once. So, he decided to marked her for series of afflictions. He caused her so many accidents, sometimes snakes could be seen on her bed physically. He even went as far as manipulating her to sleep or go to bed with her mother's husband. And the illicit relationship produced a child. At last, this evil uncle planted many evil arts in her body that will render her completely useless. But glory to God, here we came and God used us in His infinite mercy and delivered this sister.

Some witches in the came to threaten me with arrest but later became much afraid of what will follow next. Hence, they left shamefully.

Not too long, exactly nine months later, the whole witches and wizards in the land ganged up again my ministry and decided to frustrate it. As they could not harm me personally, neither any of my family members, hence they went after my church members. In three months, they threw confusion in the church and yet scattered the members. How? By polluting their minds to desert the church. I saw the shock of my life while I behold frailly how people left my ministry one after the other without any reason. How did I knew? Because when interviewed by concerned remaining members, they will relate that nothing was the cause. But I knew exactly what was the cause. Because this has already been told us in

Ephesians 6:12 For we wrestle not against flesh and blood, but against principalities, against powers, against the rulers of the darkness of this world, against spiritual wickedness in high places.

So, this is the cause because the witches and wizards in the new place also vowed to destroy my ministry.

I stood my ground and declared a spiritual war against the kingdom of darkness in the land. It wasn't easy because this was kingdom of light versus kingdom of darkness. Every of my prayer warriors left me. I became alone again. I will lead prayers, sing, preach, conduct deliverance and healing, take announcement and share the benediction. It was a daunting task but God was with me and my strength all through.

Isaiah 40:29 He giveth power to the faint; and to them that have no might he increaseth strength.

I saw yet another hell. At this point, many thoughts ran through my head, and kept asking myself lots of questions, and sometimes even God. But I remained more confident in the Holy One of Israel because He changed not; neither will He fail.

He has never failed; and He will never failed either. So, in the midst of this, I stood my ground and held onto my faith because that's the only thing that will sustain and vindicate me in the end.

Habakkuk 2:4b ....but the just shall live by his faith.

Jesus said, he who endures till the end shall be saved. So this became my guiding light and watch word.

Chapter Eleven

HERE COMES THE WORSE

It was 4:00am on Wednesday 2022, the witches in the land conspired and confederated to unleash mayhem on my household, after that I have traveled for a mission work in one interior hinterland.

They waited patiently until I traveled, then was their mission rightful to strike.

Let me confessed here that, the night before I traveled, I had a dream where God shew to me what was to come. But I was tired from midnight prayers and also overwhelmed with my journey preparations in the morning, so I gave little attention to the dream. But I contemplated much before setting out for the journey to the extend, I could not leave home on time. My host pastor was already calling to know how far I have fared with the journey, but I told him I' ll soon be on my way. I initially wanted to cancel the journey for another time but I remembered him telling me, he has done publicity and people have started flocking the venue. I had little choice but to agree on coming. I also recalled canceling the first program appointment with him, hence this second one it won't be good to do same.

Please learn this, anytime you want to do anything and your spirit is so down or reluctant, just know that it's God trying to stop you from the danger ahead. Be sensitive to heed to the warning sign. The true sign that you will know if is God speaking is that, there will be such a peace within to obey but lack of peace to disobey.

So, I started out on the journey reluctantly but I reached the place safely to the glory of God.

A day after, I received a distress call from my wife at around 11:52pm, informing me that there was a heavy down pour of rain and it ripped off the whole roof of our house completely. And that the house was immersed in water. The building is a detached bungalow that contains seven bedrooms with many toilets. I occupied the house only I and my family of five including a young male protegee or mentee of about twenty two years in the ministry. Other rooms are for visiting members.

I was caught up in a deep sleep when I received this call. After I dropped the call, five minutes later, I heard in my ears, thieves. I instantly knew it will be in my house. I wanted to call my wife back to tell her not to leave the house but I had flat battery because the place I went had no electricity for some weeks.

The young man who was supposed to be helping my wife out with reorganizing things in the house ran for his life and never came back till the next day.

My wife did her best by locking the whole house with padlocks. She went and sat down by an umbrella tree in front of the house. But concerned neighbor came and advised her to bring the children and herself to lodge in her house seeing that they were cold from the rain.

My wife took the children to sleep but later came back to sit at the usual place watching over the house, because she was not at peace to leave the place without a watch person. Meanwhile, some thieves have arrived and ready to invade the house but the presence of my wife won't let them have their way in. So, they hanged around waiting for the opportunity of silence.

Again, the neighbor who accommodated my wife and the children came to plea with her to go have some rest as the weather was too cold and it may affect her health.

Eventually my wife heed to her pressure and left the place. The thieves now have their full access and burgled the house made away with many valuables including church instruments. Because we are still in the process of building the church tent.

Hence the instruments are always kept in my house pending when we shall complete the church tent.

The total estimate of theft items was worth over five thousand dollars ($5,00).

I came back the next day in the morning only to be greeted by this colossal damage.

I was very worried and began to quarry in the spirit who perpetrated this act. I caught one suspect and took him to be remanded in the law enforcement agency custody before I will fish out the rest.

But while I was working out modalities to complete my mission of getting the rest suspects, the Spirit of the Lord asked me emphatically to stop and free the culprit in the custody and die the matter. I instantly conferred not with flesh and blood but acted exactly as I was told by the Lord.

What followed next shocked me beyond human comprehension. Many of my church members including some of my elders in church went behind gossiping about me. And this group of elders never cared to come and greet or show their sympathy till date.

I watched in amazement but not despaired because I know that my redeemer lives. And He has been gracious in supplying all our needs daily.

The church began to experience a high level of decrease in numbers.

These group of people went behind spreading evil report about our ministry but I never responded to any of them, neither was I discouraged by their act. I rather kept praying for their enlightenment and blessings.

I knew such time will come and it has come but it won't last. Satan will only try his evil best but it must be turned to our good if we stand with God. Glory!

We saw instant hatred orchestrated by Satan through some of our former members.

When some of them were been asked privately what the issues were, but they responded nothing. Only giving flimsy excuses which are not relevant to the matter at hand. Still some of the faithful members will come and explain. But my answer to them was, please leave them alone, only pray for them. If anyone thinks I offend him or her, let them come and meet with me. At least I am human as they are.

I told my members, you may not know what is going on but I knew exactly what is happening and it won't last.

Therefore be steadfast and courageous, don't faint because we're winning the battle and you shall rejoice for the salvation of our God who Has promised, 'I will not leave you nor forsake you until the end of time'.

I believe Him and that settled it!

Chapter Twelve

GOD'S GRACE

As a child of God, there's hardly anything you will do without the grace of God. I'm not an exception. Let me say that, the move of God usually causes Satan and his demons to tremble and not be at peace in their kingdom, until they strategize and come up with a means of stopping it. But glory be to God, Satan can't stand God's move no matter what he does or will do. At best, there may be temporal suspension but not permanent.

I faced gross attacks from the kingdom of darkness. They tried to attack I and my family but couldn't. They also employed so many devices but to no avail. Eventually, they turned to my members again and polluted their minds against the ministry. You may think I am exaggerating things but just be open enough to receive what I am sharing with. I don't take your trust for granted, neither will I be mean enough to tell you lies. Why am saying this is, some people are so cynical that they seem not to believe anything of sort. If you're talking of the witchcraft in Africa, may I inform you that they don't want anything to do with light i.e pertaining to God. And anything God they will fight it tooth and nail. That's why the spiritually strong churches in Nigeria which preach the true undiluted gospel are giants in prayer, and also fireful and must remain otherwise they won't last.

May I shock you! The average churches in Nigeria are being manipulated daily because Satan and his demons have craftily found their way into the church. I will give you one example, why do you see so much hatred in the Christiandom in Nigeria? That's exactly what I mean. If you stand on the ground of truth and love, Satan will manipulate other gospel preachers; I mean respected fathers and mentors not just in Nigeria only but around the world to incise and promote hatred and separatism against you. Only a few fathers of faith accommodate others with love. While the others who are after crowd gathering will openly distance themselves from other ministers and ministries claiming they're not of God. But my question is, if these supposedly so righteous preachers think others are not preaching or believing well, why not they call on their attention and preach the right gospel to them so they can repent and change?

Has the word of God changed? Hear what God says, **Amplified Bible Jeremiah 23:29-31 Is not My word like fire [that consumes all that cannot endure the test]?" says the Lord, "and like a hammer that breaks the [most stubborn] rock [in pieces]? Therefore behold (hear this), I am against the [counterfeit] prophets," says the Lord, "[I am descending on them with punishment, these prophets] who steal My words from one another [imitating the words of the true prophets]. Hear this, I am against the prophets," says the Lord, "who use their**

[own deceitful] tongues and say, 'Thus says the Lord.'

I recently heard a very disturbing statement from a well respected preacher in Nigeria on TV; who stood in the church amidst his innocent congregants in live service and declared to them and others following online that, "the Spirit of the Lord told him that the prophet who has recently gone to be with the Lord is a Sooth Sayer. Very much disturbing confusion I must say. While calling the great prophet a soothsayer, he failed to do his homework very well to ascertain who and who did the false prophet according to him impacted. Meanwhile, there is a bosom friend and a ministry associate of his that receives impartation from this prophet he claimed is a soothsayer.

Am I now to blame this minister for his ignorance? No! I know for sure it's the unfruitful work of Satan to create hatred and division.

Let me say this as the Lord impressed upon my spirit. **The day the Nigerian church will be**

united in true love, there will be massive revival all over Africa, and by extension, the world at large.

Check the statistics, the biggest churches in the world are situated more in Nigeria with an average of hundred of millions attendees weekly. This should help you to understand what I am saying.

But the simple answer is Satan at work. This is why starting up a genuine ministry is an adventure of battle upon battles in Nigeria.

I know this may also be applicable to other countries especially the Asian countries.

At this point, I invite you to put the churches of Christ Jesus in Nigeria and Africa at large in your daily prayers. We shall surely win the battle in Jesus Christ name.

Finally, I want to submit that, I and my family and the church is living and striving by God's grace.

This is my story!

Thank you for reading and following through.

CONCLUSION

In rounding up this epic story, this is the advice I will like to sell to the world, especially to the body of Christ. The scripture says, 'buy the truth and sell it not!'

As you had access to this book, please don't you trivialize what you read here. This truth is capable of shielding you from great troubles, especially to my fellow servants in the vineyard of God.

There are lessons I will like you to learn with me from this story as outlined below.

- Please and please, if you're not called into power ministry or you have not yet received grace, don't go pulling down Satanic alters. This is for your health. If there is no corresponding grace backing you, your life will be in serious danger. The witchcraft and wizardry especially in Africa is much more destructive than those in the west or foreign continents.

- When someone brings such problem and you know you cannot handle it because your grace level is not enough, please refer the person to a higher grace. Or better still take him or her there if you can. Don't even start the process because if you do, witchcraft powers will mark you out for serious attacks. Am I now advocating and invoking fear of Satan upon the body of Christ? Far from it. Not at all. But what am saying is grace level and experience. Take for instance, just as the medical science, some doctors are more experience than others by virtue of their nature, intelligence, academic qualifications, years in service and other criteria necessary. That's exactly what am trying to communicate.

- Stay in your calling. Whatever call you may have received from God to work with Him, stay in it and don't cross. Because there is great danger in crossing the boundary of your calling: for it can bring premature death. Learn from Deacon Stephen who was martyred prematurely. Yes he was anointed and filled with the Holy Ghost: but he was ordained to serve tables and not to preach. The moment he left his calling for another ministry of preaching God's word which he considered to be a higher calling; he was killed. So, learn to stay in your calling for your safety and protection.

1 Corinthians 7:20 Let every man abide in the same calling wherein he was called.

- Do not rush to enter peoples' battle, pray and seek God's permission first before you do. And that may take you seconds or minutes not necessary days or weeks depending on your grace level. But if need be for long consultation with God why not!

- Always seek deliverance from a higher grace when you noticed some anomaly within. You can get my book on this topic **"WHY IS DELIVERANCE SO IMPORTANT?"** to learn more on the issue of deliverance.

- Learn from my experience. Some ministries and churches are stagnant in growth today because of this same reason, and they lacked what next to do to come out of the situation. My advice to such ministers and ministries is; seek deliverance from higher grace and impartation. Or better still, godly counsel.

- Lastly, don't expose yourself to demonic attacks, remain prayerful and fireful and stay safe.

- Thank you.

Please if you have been blessed with this book, kindly consider supporting by making your donation to the accounts on the donation page.

Any amount is welcome! And also share with others to who wil support keep blessing souls. God will reward you mightily.

Your donations shall go a long way in helping me to keep writing and bringing free books to you.

You don't know a soul might just be won by your act of kindness.

Should in case you wish to reach me, kindly contact through these mediums

+2348029192303, +2348151887054

fredwil2013@gmail.com

PRAYERS AGAINST WITCHCRAFT MANIPULATION

Please pray this prayers angrily in your spirit.

1) O' Lord my Father, every witchcraft attacks against my life and destiny comes to an abrupt end now in Jesus matchless name.

2) My Father my fighter, arise and destroy every witchcraft manipulation against my life, family and the government of my country in Jesus Christ name.

3) I received back every of my stolen blessings from the witchcraft kingdom seven fold in Jesus mighty name.

Proverbs 6:30-31 Men do not despise a thief, if he steal to satisfy his soul when he is hungry;

But if he be found, he shall restore sevenfold; he shall give all the substance of his house.

Go ahead and celebrate your victory in Jesus Christ name.

Passionate Appeal!

Please I humbly and passionately invite your gracious support and donation to help my free books publishing. I have a passion to build a free online books for global consumption.

Please support this noble course to help pay for quality proof reading and editing before publishing.

As you do so, may you be richly blessed.

W.I Joseph

Please for more info contact

fredwil07@yahoo.com

+2348151887054

Agwan Gede Kwotto Nasarawa State - Nigeria

www.sfe.org.ng

For Support/ Donation

Use any of the below mediums convenient for you.

Perfect Money Just perfect

U38877935

E39282756

G38563264

PAYEER

P1076792383

WebMoney Sapienti sat

WMID: 285662555478

USERNAME: +2348029192303

Payoneer

fredwil2013@gmail.com

Skrill MONEY TRANSFER

advcash

fredwil2013@gmail.com

WESTERN UNION WU

Wilfred Iorhemba Joseph

fredwil2013@gmail.com

Acct Name: Wilfred Joseph Iorhemba

Acct Number: 2237953216

Bank Name: United Bank for Africa -UBA

Location: Nasarawa - Nigeria

MoneyGram money transfer

Ria MONEY TRANSFER

Wilfred Iorhemba Joseph

08029192303

Or

United Bank for Africa -UBA

Bank code: 033362087

Nasarawa - Nigeria

Please if you use Western Union, MoneyGram or Ria, endeavor to send me your donation details through this email fredwil2013@gmail.com

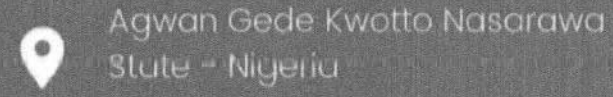

OTHER BOOKS BY THE AUTHOR

- **THE POWERS OF THE FOUR WINDS:**

How to Harness and Optimize this Force

- **WHY IS DELIVERANCE SO IMPORTANT?**

Your Greatest Advantage in the Battles of Life

- **KINGDOM KEYS FOR WINNING BATTLES**

Creating Possibilities Where Impossibilities Exist

- **HOW TO FULFILL YOUR DESTINY**

A Top Niche You'll Ever Need

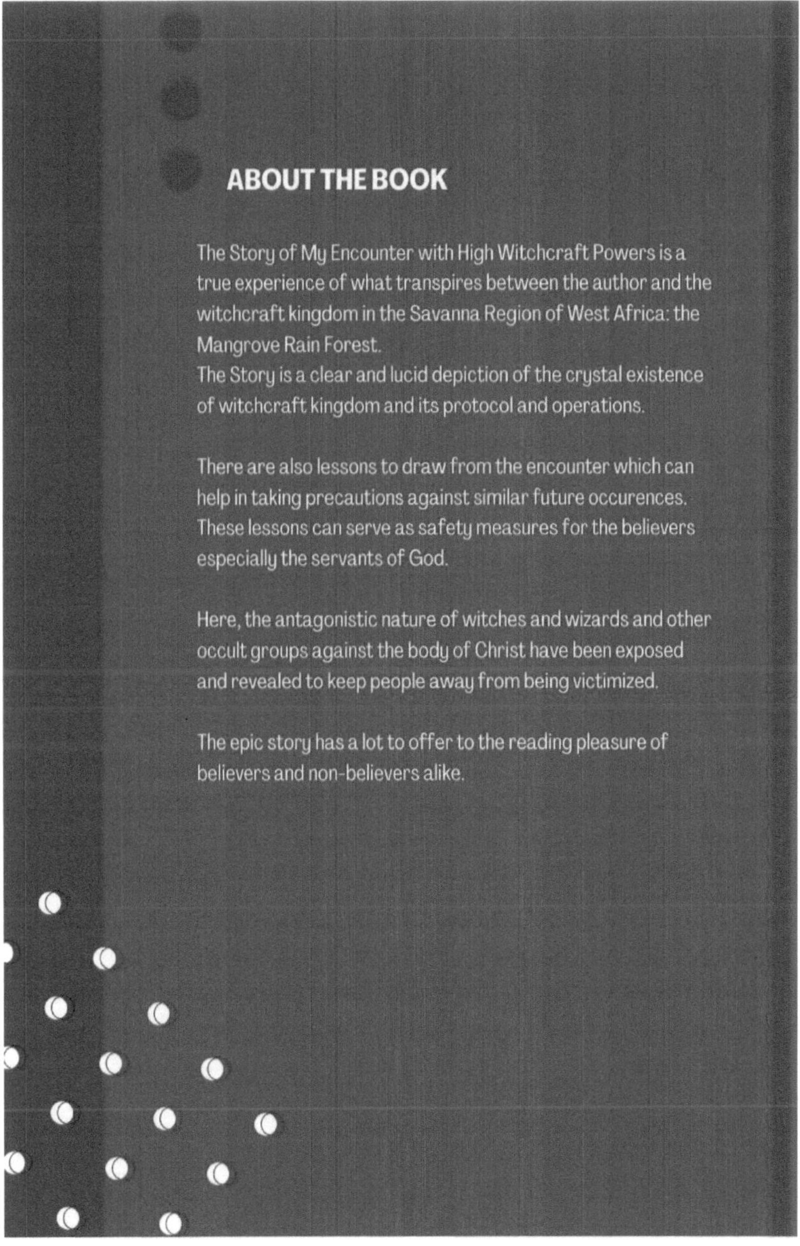

ABOUT THE BOOK

The Story of My Encounter with High Witchcraft Powers is a true experience of what transpires between the author and the witchcraft kingdom in the Savanna Region of West Africa: the Mangrove Rain Forest.
The Story is a clear and lucid depiction of the crystal existence of witchcraft kingdom and its protocol and operations.

There are also lessons to draw from the encounter which can help in taking precautions against similar future occurences. These lessons can serve as safety measures for the believers especially the servants of God.

Here, the antagonistic nature of witches and wizards and other occult groups against the body of Christ have been exposed and revealed to keep people away from being victimized.

The epic story has a lot to offer to the reading pleasure of believers and non-believers alike.

www.ingramcontent.com/pod-product-compliance
Lightning Source LLC
LaVergne TN
LVHW040948150826
845672LV00002B/594

9798847500821